Couples and the Art of Playing

Couples and the Art of Playing

❖

Three Easy and Enjoyable Ways to Nurture and Heal Relationships

Keith Hackett,
M.A., D.Min.
Diplomate AAPC
Clinical Member AAMFT

http://www.KeithHackett.net

iUniverse, Inc.
New York Lincoln Shanghai

Couples and the Art of Playing
Three Easy and Enjoyable Ways to Nurture and Heal Relationships

iUniverse, Inc.

For information address:
iUniverse, Inc.
2021 Pine Lake Road, Suite 100
Lincoln, NE 68512
www.iuniverse.com

ISBN: 0-595-29102-3 (pbk)
ISBN: 0-595-65963-2 (cloth)

Printed in the United States of America

Contents

Preface

We have made life complicated!! Books, workshops on how to improve your cooking skills, financial management skills, health care skills, and many other skills. We have done the same with marriage. How have we survived for so long without these tools? Many of the books are long, use complicated language and theories, and are expensive. In my psychotherapy practice I try to simplify—go for the least possible effort and cost to accomplish a goal. I try to go for what is realistic and manageable for people rather than the ideal. Ask for less and you get less is not always true! If you want to talk for forty minutes and your partner only wants to talk for ten then you have already agreed upon ten minutes so go for that, rather than argue for forty and end up with nothing.

This book is short, inexpensive, readable, understandable, and easy to apply. If you enjoy reading long complicated books this will be a snap for you. If you don't like reading, then hopefully this won't be a big chore, and it might even be fun and helpful—give it a try.

Over the twenty-five plus years of my clinical practice I have acquired many concepts and techniques that I have adapted to fit my style and my beliefs. I have added some of my own. This book is my attempt to take you into the office of one marital therapist and to share with you some of my insights. It is not intended to replace therapy if therapy is needed, but I do believe that it can be a very valuable boost to therapy, for both clients and therapists.

Case studies have gone through the usual editing and name changing to protect confidentiality.

I use the term "marriage" frequently and ask you to read this as a simple and less clumsy way of referring to any committed relationship—whether heterosexual or homosexual. I am aware that some people are denied the benefits of marriage, and others choose to live "as if" without the legal ceremony. People in any form of committed relationship can use the ideas that I will be presenting. They are, I believe, essential concepts for those contemplating or starting a life together to establish right away. The earlier a concept is learned the sooner it becomes a habit.

My wife Joan and I have together tested what is in this book and found that most of the concepts have worked for us most of the time. We hope they will work for you—you will probably have to adapt them, as any book like this one is basically saying what works for the author and rarely fits exactly for all of the readers. Be creative—make it work for you! A few years ago I wrote an article for our agency that was entitled "Would You Remarry Your Spouse?" For me the answer was always a very loud "**yes**". The reason—Joan has been and is today my playmate.

Acknowledgments

There are many people I can thank for helping bring this book to fruition. First, to my parents who birthed and nurtured me and showed me for over eighteen years of living with them what a happy marriage can be like. Second, to our children Conrad, Joanne and Thomas who taught me much that is not contained in books. Thirdly, to David and Vera Mace who trained and mentored Joan and me in Marriage Enrichment and who were good friends to us when we lived in North Carolina. Also to my various supervisors—to Wynn and Marjorie at the Marriage Guidance Council in England; to Ted, Charlie, Wes and Mac at the Dept. of Pastoral Counseling, N.C. Baptist Hospital in Winston-Salem; and here to Jack and Loris and to our agency consultants Gordon and Don. To all who did some editing, especially my brother-in-law, Richard Elcock, and Sallirae Henderson, who believed in me and what I have to say and who encouraged me when I felt like giving up. Mostly, thanks to my playmate of over thirty-five years, Joan, whom I have been happily married to for over thirty-three years.

Thanks also to Abingdon Press for their permission to develop the ideas of David and Vera Mace as exemplified in their book *How to Have a Happy Marriage,* 1977, and other similar books.

1

Is Communication Really the Problem?

John and Susan's Story

John and Susan came in for counseling complaining that they didn't know how to communicate with each other. They had been married for eight years and had two boys, five and four, and a girl, three. Both of them had been through alcoholism treatment six years ago and had maintained sobriety. Both were involved in A.A. and in their church, and were busy with their careers, as well as trying to raise their children so they would be healthy, well adjusted adults. They desperately wanted to learn how to communicate—they wanted to do it 'right'! They were dedicated to each other, to their programs, to God, and to their children. Both of them were very serious about wanting to learn how to communicate correctly. One of their other problems was that sex had always been a cause of tension between them. A concern for Susan was that she had never been orgasmic.

I asked them the question that I was taught in graduate school not to ask—"Why? Why do you want to learn to communicate?" John and Susan told me that both of them believed that if they learned to do that then they would have a really good relationship, and then everything else would be fine. "If we learned to communicate then we would be better spouses, parents, and friends."

Towards the end of the session I told them that I didn't think that poor communication was their major problem. They told me (as have most couples I have worked with) that when they first met, they talked

1

about everything again and again. They were friends, good friends—then they became husband and wife, and then parents. I suggested to them that what they needed to do was to become friends again and not to concentrate on learning to communicate (which really is a stuffy way to say "talk") because, from what they had "communicated" to me, they already knew how to do that—they had just dropped the habit of doing it.

What do we do to become friends again? Is it not by learning to talk better with each other? I explained that I had some ideas about how they could become friends and asked if they would be willing to try what I was about to suggest. They agreed even before I explained what it was. Before the next session I suggested they do something fun. They were instructed to play together, just the two of them, no children and with no other adults. Not the kind of homework that people expect to be given when they come to marriage counseling to learn to better communicate.

Problem:—they both came from alcoholic families. Each was the eldest of their families and each had taken on the role of substitute parent by eight years of age. Because of the large amount of dysfunction in their families neither had completed high school, and they had married each other when they were eighteen. They both knew how to be serious—very serious, but they had no idea how to play. I was prepared for this, and so I suggested that they modify my instructions, and for the first time, ask their children to show them and teach them how to play.

They came to their next session excited and hopeful, and they announced that they were now friends, and even better than friends! Here's what they told me had happened.

It was a wet Saturday morning in October. They got the children together and told them that they needed their help. Mommy and Daddy were seeing someone to help them get along better and this man, their counselor, wanted them to play but they didn't know how to. They told the children that they had promised their counselor that they would do whatever the children suggested. "No kidding," said the eldest. "No kidding," they both said, now with some trepidation as they listened to the tone of their son's voice.

The three children took a few minutes and then announced that they wanted a family mud pie fight. Mom and Dad both knew what that meant and they really weren't too keen—but they had promised. Now remember this is a serious couple, and so the first task is for everyone to find their oldest and worst clothes and change into them—they nearly ruined the fun even before they had started! Usually they did not give the children so much control.

Well, for the next twenty minutes, wearing old clothes, they made mud pies and threw them at each other. They covered each other in mud, they ran around, they chased each other, and they laughed like they hadn't laughed in a long time. They threw and they got hit. And John and Susan became like children. Then they got the hose and buckets of water and they soaked each other to get the mud off—but they got carried away and chased each other around with the water and the mud fight turned into a water fight.

This is a serious couple that previously would not have believed they knew how to have a spontaneous water fight, after a planned mud fight. And they would never have agreed to a mud fight if they had not been setup for it by their counselor.—Perhaps in the future they will be more careful about what they agree to before they know what it is!

Susan and John gave the children a warm shower and then left them to watch the Saturday morning cartoons. They went to their bedroom and as they were having a shower together (something they rarely had time or inclination to do), they found themselves spontaneously making love. One of the other problems that this couple had shared with me was that sex had always been a problem for them. Among other issues, Susan had not been orgasmic since they had married. Sex had become an obligation for each of them. That morning they lost themselves and they discovered themselves. Having learned to play like children, they now played as adults and what play it was! They forgot about the children—about the serious business of being parents—and

Susan had not one but three orgasms and John enjoyed being able to go slower and be more attentive to Susan's needs—they had sex—they made love.

Two sessions and a follow-up three months later and they were doing fine. They described themselves as having become friends who played often without the help or presence of the children. And yes, they are talking ("communicating") just fine. They are resolving a number of old disagreements and continuing to struggle with others. And all without any more help from me.

Diane and Robert's Story

Another couple, Diane and Robert, came in with a similar problem. They had been married for twenty years and had two daughters, 15 and 17. They hadn't been getting along as a couple and were wondering what would happen to them when the two girls left home. They didn't seem to have much in common except the girls. They were both busy in their individual careers; one was an attorney and the other a doctor. They were active in different civic and religious organizations, and in their daughters' lives. Many of their friends described them as "the ideal family." The homework that I gave them was to go away by themselves for a weekend—I emphasized the obvious. By themselves means without the girls! You see, this couple (and they are not unusual in this regard) had not had one day by themselves as a couple since the first girl had been born, let alone an overnight. Everything they did they did as a family. They had taken very seriously the challenge of the sixties to raise healthy children, and to let them know in words and actions that they are loved—and not to miss any of the children's events. The weekend I defined for them began after work on Friday and ended as late as possible on Sunday evening. They were to go away and relax and play—and they were to absolutely avoid any heavy conversations, and they were, under no circumstances, to discuss their problems or to talk about the girls.

They came back to see me two weeks later beaming like newlyweds. They had rediscovered each other at the coast as they walked on the beach, went around the shops, ate at quaint restaurants, and relaxed in the hot tub in their room. They kept the rules until they stopped at a restaurant on the way home. Over the evening meal that started at seven-thirty, they felt so at ease with each other that they brought up a number of issues and talked them through really well. A few other issues surfaced and they agreed to disagree but without the old hostility. And a few others that came up. Well, they had to leave them until another time because the restaurant people wanted to close and go home. Prior to checking out of their motel, they had booked another weekend for six months later.

2

The Key

In the past thirty years almost every couple that I have counseled started by telling me that they didn't communicate very well with each other. One couple was even sent to me by a psychologist who told them that she was unable to help them until they learned to communicate. It was my task to teach them and then I was to send them back to her for ongoing therapy. I asked them who made the appointment and she said that she did, and then I asked him how he knew about it and he said she told him. "But," I said, "you don't communicate." "No," they both replied. I inquired how they got to my office and he said he drove them here, and so I asked her how she knew to come with him and she said she just did. Again I said, "You don't communicate", and again they both replied, "No." We went through a few exchanges before it dawned that, "Oh, we do communicate, don't we?" I clarified that yes, they did, in fact, communicate—probably not very well, but yes they did communicate. The fact that they communicated badly was far better news than that they did not communicate at all. Maybe communication wasn't the basic problem after all.

So I began to wonder, "What is the key?"

What Do Couples Do?

Virtually all of these couples told me that when they first met, before they got married, they talked a great deal about almost everything—and that was one of the big reasons why they married. Now I must admit that it took me quite a few years before I really heard couples telling me this. Early in my career, as soon as couples said that they "couldn't communicate" I would go into my teaching mode or put them in one of our classes, and then proceed to teach them what they already knew, only now it was packaged in a more technical (complicated) manner. Then they would try to learn 'communication skills,' and session after session we would practice them, and occasionally a few of the skills would work, but often not for very long. And then there were the couples that now had something else to argue about—the correct technical way to communicate. Some did communicate better but their relationship was still not much improved. I became frustrated—what was I doing wrong? What was I missing? Why, when people could communicate better, were many of them still not getting along very well?

David Mace, one of the first executive directors of the American Association for Marriage and Family Therapy and founder with his wife Vera of the Association for Couples in Marriage Enrichment, in a private conversation sometime in 1979, once shared with me that when he had a couple in his office who were arguing he felt hopeful for them. But when he had a couple who sat as far from each other as they could, rarely looked at each other, and one or both of them had little to say, then he was not very hopeful for them. Arguing, he went on to say, may be a positive indication that counseling may help the couple to develop a healthier relationship. Apathy usually means that the couple has waited too long to obtain the help they needed. When two people are arguing they are making contact with each other. The challenge now comes to help them to turn this negative contact into positive contact. If teaching them to communicate better and argue less doesn't do it—what could?

So what should I do? Go back to the basics—what did I learn in my first counseling class? Listen, listen, and listen even more. What were my clients telling me that was distinct from what I wanted to hear? I began to practice the ancient art of fully listening. What were couples telling me? "When we first met we talked about everything."

I began to hear this from couple after couple who now said they didn't know how to communicate. Apparently they used to know how to talk to each other, but now for some reason they weren't doing it. I began to ask them what else they did when they first met, and often up until they got married, and in a few cases, even up until the first child was born. No big surprise here. I found out that they dated. But what did this mean? It meant that **they played, they had fun, they were friends, they spent time together,** and often it was just the two of them. Some told me of the frequent hikes they used to go on. Others of dances they went to. Couples shared how they would hang out at the park and throw a Frisbee or a ball, or just sit and relax; pack a picnic and spend time at the lake or at the beach; go swimming; go to a movie or rent a movie; go to the theatre or a concert; go out for a meal or have a special meal at one of their favorite places; go skiing—snow and water; take trips and many other events.

Just asking about how they met began the process of positive change. Couples come in to counseling arguing, blaming and accusing, and I usually listen to this for around twenty minutes, often wondering why they are still together. Then I ask them to tell me how they met and most begin to relax, their voice tones soften and some even smile and laugh. Their past was good and it can be used to create hope for their future. We talk about dates and play and so their homework is to go and play, and many leave the first session with a new sense of hope.

What Do Children Do?

Then I moved my attention from clients to children and I discovered the same dynamic as I observed them. Children become friends by playing together, not by discussing the theories of the universe, or by sorting out their compatibility, or by taking friendship tests to see if they should be together. They don't worry if they are doing it correctly according to the latest best-seller on how each gender is supposed to relate. And if they have a falling-out, they don't debrief the problem and try to lay the blame and spend ages in counseling. No, they just go back out and "wanna play" and play they do—and play makes friends, and play resolves a lot of conflicts and falling-outs.

As children become adolescents we begin to teach them how to become adults.—This means learning how to hang on to conflicts, and finding someone to blame and not making up until the other person apologizes—and it needs to be a sincere apology! Jesus said we cannot enter the Kingdom of Heaven unless we become like children. Maybe the same could be said of marriage—maybe we cannot have healthy marriages unless we become like children—at least in the area of play.

Babies, I believe, are born with two basic drives or needs: the need to be loved and the need for attention. We know that for a baby to develop in a healthy way, emotionally and physically, s/he needs to be nurtured, touched, held, hugged, kissed, and talked to. The baby from an early age needs to experience **PLAY.** Other children and adults develop a play language, and they buy all kinds of age appropriate toys with which to connect with the infant. Even people who would not usually describe themselves as playful usually manage to play with babies.

What about babies and children who do not experience much love-play from those around? For these little persons the attention drive kicks in, and we discover that s/he knows how to create combat-play. The baby cries and throws a tantrum, and the child continues that behavior, and also uses or refuses food as a weapon and regresses in toilet skills, and thus gets attention. Unfortunately it is not good attention, and as in most combat-play situations, it does not lead to a healthy relationship. In the extreme, the lack of love-play resulting in combat-play can lead to various forms of child abuse, including battering the baby or child to death.

What Do Nations Do?

This concept of love-play or combat-play is not restricted to families but is written about in every history book. The ancient Greeks knew this. According to a pamphlet that I purchased when in Greece:

"The Olympia, or Olympic Games as they are now called, were associated with the ideals of noble rivalry and peace, and for many centuries they forged the national unity of the ancient Greek world."[1]

In the eighth century B.C., a law was passed that stated that all wars and hostilities between the Greek states should cease for the duration of the games. For various reasons the Games were not held from the fourth century A.D. until 1896. Since 1896 they have been held, following the ancient tradition, every four years, and from 1936 onwards

"the Olympic Flame has been carried to the Games as a symbol of peace, friendship and brotherhood among people."[2]

Winning in the Olympic Games can replace conquest by war; love-play or game-play can replace combat-play. Nations today are still very competitive and count the number of medals that their athletes win. Even at the height of the Cold War both the USSR and the USA competed in the Olympics.

PLAY then is at the heart of our very being; it is one of our first activities. Play is the means whereby babies, children and adults make contact with each other. My brother-in-law is a triplet and when they were three years-old their parents were concerned that they weren't "communicating" the adult way. They consulted their pediatrician whose comment was, "Why should they when they have each other to play with and talk to?"

What Did I Learn?

Because of my listening and reflecting I began to change the way that I worked with couples. What I began to discover was that often spouses

---

1. *Olympia,* Olympic Publications, Theo. Agridiotis, Skoufa 56—Athens 106 72, 1994, p. 1
2. Ibid, p. 2

do not do a very good job of communicating; parents do slightly better, at least about the children; but it is friends who are the best communicators. I was encouraged in my discovery by the work of John Gottman and his colleagues who, after studying several thousand volunteer research couples over a period of sixteen years, challenged the idea that communication is the key to good relationships and romance. At the heart of their research is that couples need to continually develop their friendship, playfulness and affirmation of each other.[3] [4] [5]

About the same time that Gottman began his research I was also beginning to develop my theories based upon my observations. Maybe, I began to think, **maybe the key to a creative and healthy marriage is to develop the art of friendship, and maybe the key to friendship is to become 'play-mates'**…No, that can't be, that sounds far too simple an answer for a complicated problem…. Well, try it first. Read on.

3.   John M. Gottman and Nan Silver, *The Seven Principles for Making Marriage Work,* (Three Rivers Press, 1999), p. 8

4.   Ibid, p. 19

5.   *The Relationship Cure,* (Crown Publishing Group, 2001), p. 28

CONCEPT

Before

Talk

There

Was

Play

THE PROGRAM

When Joan and I married we were living in England. I was involved in church work and Joan was teaching in a comprehensive school for 11–18 year-olds. We decided that we needed at least half a day each week doing something fun together; not shopping or cleaning house, as much fun as those things can be—we wanted to do something quite different. This sounded reasonable and should be no problem. Well, it was a problem. Tuesday after school finished was a good time for me but not for Joan—she had a regular school meeting on Tuesday evenings. Friday after school was a good time for Joan but not for me—I had a regular youth group on Friday nights. Saturdays I either had a wedding or it was chores and shopping. And Sundays I was always preaching morning and evening, and often in the afternoon as well.

So what happened to this great idea? We argued over when to do it and we each blamed the other when we didn't do it. Then we went from the IDEAL to the REALISTIC. We took out our calendars and found half a day each month, and we wrote it in our calendars in nonerasable ink. I didn't like feeling controlled by the calendar and planning it in this way. But think about it. We planned it that way when we were dating and it worked fine so maybe it will work after marriage also. Guess what? It not only worked, but we also discovered that when we committed to half a day a month we often found other times opening up. These were bonuses that led to a lot less arguing and blaming. A colleague, Frank Picard, gave me another way to consider the use of the calendar: the Seven Ps—Proper Prior Planning Prevents P (....) Poor Performance!

I discovered through the above experience:

We waste time arguing and blaming when we don't take time to play.

Here is the program's minimum outline:

1) Play

    a) One date of two to three hours every month.

    b) One weekend away together every year.

    c) One week away together every five years.

2) Playful Sharing

    "5 and 5" every day.

3) Positive Playful Manipulation

    How to be playful every day

3

Play

1) **One date of two to three hours every month**

To get this part of the program started, I suggest that for two months you try to do an intensive alternate dating program, every week. Here is how this works:

Agree to a two to three hour time each week. It is easier to do this if you can commit to the same time each week. If one or both of you works alternating shifts then plan your date times in advance and put them on your calendars (or whatever you need to do so that you do not forget!). Toss a coin—whoever gets heads goes first. This saves a lot of arguing about who will go first, and then never doing it. Let's say it's the husband. He gets to plan anything, any date he wants, except something that he knows his wife would absolutely hate. Taking her fishing (his favorite thing to do) may not be the best thing to start with. So, if he is not sure about something—whether she would like it or not—then this may be the time to plan that date. He is not trying to plan a date he thinks she would thoroughly enjoy because if he gets it wrong then it is spoiled. To add fun to the date I suggest that they treat this as if they are single and this is an encounter with a new person they have just met and all they know about that person is what s/he does not like. Her deal is to go along with whatever he has planned and treat it like a date with a new guy. She is to try her hardest to enjoy it just like couples do when they are dating—and if she isn't enjoying it then she is to fake it, just like couples do when they are first dating. After the date neither asks the other if they enjoyed it (this is what I call "the banned question") because at that point they revert back to the "honesty" of husband and wife. We wait two months for this part of the program.

Next week we reverse the roles, same rules. Oh, and by the way, planning the dates means ALL of the planning including arranging for the baby-sitter, etc.

A few additional guidelines and recommendations

This is a date for just the two of you. It is not a family event, nor is it to be spent with other people. I am amazed how many times I have to very carefully and slowly spell this out to couples that I am working with, and then I have to answer questions as to whether I really do mean only the two of them! Yes, I do mean that—that is what a date is! No, you don't take the baby, the cat or the dog with you. I remember one couple that took the dogs and went to the park and spent most of the time arguing as to whether the dogs should be on the long leashes or free to run around.

For two to three hours the two of you will be just the two of you. It often takes one to two hours to begin to relax with each other, especially if life has been tense for some time before. Do not take more than three hours initially as you may ruin it by getting into an argument.

Being perceptive, you tell me that this is going to cost money. Yes, but a date does not necessarily have to cost a lot. And, by the way, probably not as much as you are spending on counseling and certainly nowhere near as much as a divorce and dating someone else would cost. **You are each worth every penny that you spend**. But it doesn't have to cost a lot (see chapter seven for tips on how to reduce childcare and other costs). Simple dates like going for walks in the neighborhood don't have to cost anything at all. Dates can be at home. If you have young children, let them go to the sitter's home and you can have an uninterrupted date in your own home. You don't have to wait until the children are grown and left home to have a night of wild passion—or, at least two to three hours worth.

I recommend that the date be fun, playful and interactive (see chapter six for ideas). I do not recommend going out for a meal because that tends to involve too much talking (or arguing), and usually ends up being serious and not fun. Another interesting thought: dinner out may be something to do by yourself, and then you can really enjoy the food without having to worry about the conversation. Also, I do not recommend going to a movie for exactly the opposite reason—you both will likely zone out and ignore each other and again you might as well be there by yourself. Some couples helped me to add that this also means not renting a movie and having take-out at home. Dinners and movies are things that you can do in addition to the dates. Try to avoid alcohol or other mood-altering substances just before and during the date.

At the end of two months make a list of all the dates. You each have a red pen and can put a line through any date that either of you did not enjoy—no need to discuss it (unless you really have to) or create conflict. Then select a time each month and reserve it on your calendars and put a different event (from the list that neither of you has put a line through) by each monthly commitment (date). This is a sacred commitment of your time to be shared with your partner. Nothing will cause you to break this commitment. This is another place where couples nearly always argue with me and try to convince me that I didn't mean what I just said. What if the children have something at school, or work wants me to do overtime, or Aunt Sally, whom we have never seen before, is flying into the local airport at that very time and we have to go and meet her? Politely, I ask them two things: "Do you know what an emergency is?" Then I explain that you can only deal with one emergency at a time. Then I ask them: "If you had to attend your spouse's funeral, would anything prevent you from attending?" I then assure them that these dates need even more consideration than do emergencies and funerals. And when you say no to something else, I suggest that you tell your partner and get a few extra strokes. We all feel good when our partner puts us first—in front of work, the kids, the neighbors, etc. We did this when we were dating and I hear people putting affairs before everything. We need to reclaim the priority of marriage! What a great way to build self-esteem and to show each other how really important we are to each other.

Where did we learn this?

Joan and I learned some of this from an older couple that we knew in England. Ken was a Methodist minister and Judith was his wife. I was beginning my vocation as a Methodist minister. We were visiting them and the conversation got around to what they had learned in thirty-five years of marriage and being in the ministry—how do you survive both ministry and marriage and grow? Amongst what they told us was this incident. One of the things that had attracted Judith to Ken was his absolute honesty, and she still liked that about him but sometimes it also annoyed her. She told us that in the first fifteen years of their marriage they had only occasionally had a day a week off together and often their vacations were cut short because of some church "emergency" for which Ken had to return. One Christmas she gave Ken a date book and when he opened it he discovered that every Friday had a line through it and Judith had written in funeral. He was puzzled and asked her to explain the meaning of this. She told him that she had noticed that if he had a phone call asking if he was doing anything on Thursday morning, he would look in his date book and if nothing was in there (or if they were planning to do something) he would say "no" and would then agree to whatever he was being asked to do. She also noticed that sometimes he would respond, "Oh, I have a funeral to conduct then." He conducted funerals for the local funeral director for people who did not belong to a church, and rarely would the other person ask whose funeral it was. "So now," she told him, "when someone asks if you are doing anything on Friday, you can say honestly, 'oh, I have a funeral down for Friday.'" So they began to get their days off.

Of course being an honest guy, it wasn't long before Ken explained their method to people, but by then the members of the church had begun to respect their need for a day off.

The banned question

Now, what about the question that we banned at the end of the date: "Did you enjoy it?" As you make the list and eliminate the dates neither of you enjoyed, you are answering that question. You are also doing what I think is one of the simplest and most fun tests of compatibility. If you cannot find any date that you both enjoyed then the strong likelihood is that you are incompatible and maybe this is the underlying reason why you are not getting along and arguing so much. So what do you do? Well, you consult a very experienced and skilled marital therapist or you may look at how to end the relationship with the least amount of pain. Or jump ahead and read chapter ten. Fortunately, this rarely happens.

We have now established the minimum requirement. One fun date of two to three hours every month—just for the two of you, and put it on the calendar. More dates are encouraged and one every week is the ideal. The other dates in the month could include meals and movies and maybe one or two of them could be with other people. But the number one priority is:

TWO TO THREE HOURS OF PLAY EVERY MONTH AS A COUPLE!

- At least one date a month (preferably one a week).
- Interactive play (not meals or movies).
- Only the two of you.
- Decide a regular (if possible) two to three hour period.
- Toss a coin—winner plans the date (not what your partner would hate).

- Alternate the planning.
- Both intentionally try to enjoy the date (pretend it is with a new person).
- At the end of two months evaluate.
- Put future date times (at least once a month) in the calendar for the year.
- Keep the commitment.

2) One weekend (two days) away together every year

At least once a year it is good to get away together alone. Again, let me explain that alone really does mean without other people—not even the children. What do I mean by a weekend? It will start Friday after work and go until Sunday as late as possible (or other days to fit if you work a non-traditional week). Camping, motel, resort, short cruise, or if money is tight, arrange for friends or family to come and stay at your house and you go to their house. Arrange with them beforehand that you will disengage their phone—you know the reason for that by now.

Our experience

Joan and I spent our first year after we were married living in a seminary in the San Francisco area. I was studying and Joan inquired at the seminary job center for a job. The result was a job for both of us. We spent most of the year house-sitting and looking after children ranging in age from six months to sixteen years. We had assignments that went from two days to one month. At first, being newlyweds and having no children, we were very surprised that couples would go away without their children. Then we began to observe the families before and afterwards. It was truly amazing to us. People were transformed. Both children and parents enjoyed the breaks from each other and then they were pleased to reconnect. How different from a few days earlier when most of these people seemed tired with each other and were bickering and not all that happy to be together as a family. We saw families revitalized and ready for the next step of their journey together. We were grateful for this extracurricular class and for what we had learned from it. If/when we had children, we knew one of the things that we had to do for ourselves in order to be good parents.

Back to the basics

We prepare for the marital journey by dating. Often we need to go back to the preparation stage. We need to remind ourselves that we were a couple before we were a family. I hear many people just waiting, often impatiently, for the day when their children leave home and it will be just them again. This to me is very sad, because we can have both now—it just takes carefully applying the seven Ps. The youngsters pick up these negative vibes and look for new friends and situations where they can feel more loved and accepted! Further, if all the adults have done has focused on family events, then what happens when the last child leaves home?

I am frustrated and pained when I hear of a couple getting a divorce and other people express surprise because "they were such a wonderful family." I have come not to hear this as a compliment but as a concern. For often it means that their lives at home have centered on their offspring. So what happens when that last child leaves home? David and Jennifer told me, "We knew what to do as Bethany and Diane's Dad and Mom. The girls determined our activities—school, church, sports and dance. But now they aren't here." They went on to explain that he was Bethany and Diane's Dad and she was their Mom, but who were they to each other? When Diane went off to college, they discovered that they had drifted apart as a couple and didn't even know it! How were they to reconnect—could they reconnect? I took them back to the preparation stage. In their case, we started with the weekend away rather than the weekly date.

Why did I suggest they start with the weekend rather than the weekly date? They were a very motivated and committed couple and they were presenting being stuck and lost in their relationship. They told me. "We don't know what has happened to us, but we don't seem to have anything in common any more. We don't argue but we don't have much to talk about. We want to see if we can rediscover what we used to have." They weren't blaming each other and they were both open to change. The weekend seemed appropriate for them. For the majority of couples that I work with this is not the case—they would not be able to sustain a weekend without ruining it by arguing and blaming. Because I don't know you, the reader, I would recommend starting with the weekly dates even if you are not blaming. My guess is that I only start with the weekend with one out of a hundred couples.

Extra tips

Another way that Joan and I have squeezed in an extra weekend is by taking a few extra days at the end of conferences or meetings where one person's travel, room and board is covered. Sometimes finding two for one airfares and using other cost saving strategies adds to the fun.

Many couples today have weekends without children because the children are with the non-custodial parent. Carefully coordinate visitations if you are both divorced with children so that all the children are gone the same weekend. Use some of these weekends to enjoy playing at home! Don't always use them doing household chores and shopping. Children may go to camps and weekend retreats with the church or sporting events. These are all excellent opportunities for you to have a weekend away.

- Friday after work to late Sunday night (modify for different schedules).
- Only the two of you.
- Adapt to your financial situations.

<u>3) One Week Away Together Every Five Years</u>

As part of our house-sitting, we had some couples that went away for a week or more, and again we observed how much more revitalized they were, and so we added this learning to our ideas for the future. So I strongly recommend that every three to five years couples take at least one week's vacation—just the two of you—using similar guidelines to what I have given you for the weekend.

This part of the program is optional. It's a bonus. It's like dessert. Right now it may not sound very possible or realistic. However, when you are successfully doing the other parts of the program, you will not be all that surprised to discover how easily this can happen.

- An option—bonus.
- Only the two of you.
- Pamper yourselves.

CONCEPT

Couples

Who

Play

Together

Stay

Together

4

Playful Sharing

Now that we have taken time to play and become friends once again, we can also pick up with our conversations. I want to offer you a simple and playful way to do this which is called **"5 and 5"** and, to help you establish a habit of regular sharing, I recommend that you do this every day. It is an adaptation from Marriage Encounter's "10 and 10," and from David and Vera Mace's "Daily Dialogue."[1] It is also what I call Communication 101 and is the art of mutual monologue. One of the many things that I have observed over thirty years of working with couples is that many couples attempt stage two before they have grasped stage one. They are poor at dialogue because they have not really mastered monologue. We need to learn the basic skills of sharing and listening before we can continue with discussing and then arguing.

As close as possible to each of you getting home, set aside ten minutes when you know that you will not be interrupted. This should not be over a meal as the very act of eating is distracting and can interrupt good sharing and listening. If you have children then make sure they are busy or can amuse themselves for ten minutes—and get them to answer the phone and take messages or put the answering machine on (or whatever device you use), or just turn the ringer off.

Toss a coin, and this time it is the wife who wins (remember the husband won the toss for planning the first date). The person who starts the sharing is responsible for making sure **"5 and 5"** happens. Sit where you are both comfortable and are able to look at each other.

---

1.   David and Vera Mace *How to Have a Happy Marriage*, (Abingdon, 1977), p. 65f, 127f.

Some couples like to begin by holding hands and having a moment of prayer—either silent or spoken. I prefer silent prayer here and then neither partner will feel coerced by the spoken prayer of the other. Have an alarm that you can set for five minutes and put it where neither of you can see but where you can both hear it when it rings.

Now the wife has five minutes to share her day with her husband in any way that she wishes. She can talk about what she has been doing, share conversations she has had with other people, memories that have been reactivated for her, maybe share her reflections on last night's conversation. If she finishes after three minutes then they sit quietly together until the alarm sounds-she cannot give her unused time away. If when the alarm sounds, she hasn't finished her sharing too bad—all she gets is five minutes. She will have to learn to condense her sharing in the future. This is very important as this is only a commitment for ten minutes, and we need to honor our commitments. All this time the husband is listening quietly. He can interrupt her only to clarify something that he does not fully understand. Maybe she says that she has had lunch with Vickie and she has five friends called Vickie. If he tries to figure out which one it is then he will not listen to the rest of what she is saying very attentively. So he interrupts her (for the purpose of clarification) and asks "Vickie who?" and she tells him and then she continues with her sharing.

At the end of five minutes, they change roles but there is an additional rule for the second person. He cannot respond to or share on the same topic that she has already addressed. The reason is simple: most of us do not listen well because we are often preparing our response to what we think the other person is saying or is about to say. In fact, we are often waiting for a breath in which to interrupt them and correct them or argue with them. If I cannot respond then maybe I can really learn to listen. And if I listen to all that is said then maybe I will not always need to respond because what I hear may actually be quite different from what I thought I was going to hear. It might indeed be something that I agree with, or it might end up being something quite flattering about me!

Next day the other person is responsible for making sure that **"5 and 5"** happens, and goes first. So you continue alternating the responsibility for initiating and starting. This way neither of you has to worry if your partner forgets. All you have to worry about is when it is your responsibility. If your partner forgets then the following day you simply make sure it happens!

One couple's experience

Bethany and Robert told me that the **"5 and 5"** gave them a simple structure that was short, compact and did not need a lot of thinking about. It was fairly easy to apply. They could use it if either of them had had a good or bad day. And if one of them was angry with the other, it meant that the recipient of the anger only had to listen for five minutes, not all night. In the past they had both become upset when the other interrupted which both felt justified in doing as they thought the other had finished. This is a common problem among couples. "Now," said Bethany, "when the alarm sounds I know it is my turn to speak. Until then I listen. A few days ago, Robert began his sharing by reflecting on a disagreement we had had previously. He said that I had implied something that was not true. In the past I would have interrupted and rudely corrected him, which would have led to another row. This time, following the guidelines, I just continued to listen and he went on to say that he had bounced it off a few friends at work, and he came to realize that maybe he had misunderstood me but had not bothered to check that out. And, even more remarkable (she had a twinkle in her eye as she shared this part) he said that maybe I, Robert, was wrong." I have heard many similar stories from couples that have found that by really listening without being allowed to respond immediately, they have become more able to listen non-defensively and non-judgmentally. And some for 'the first time' heard their partner say that maybe s/he was wrong. Interrupting and correcting often results in the first person retreating to their original position and defending it even if s/he had begun to change their mind.

Now here are a few additional guidelines and recommendations.

1) Often at the end of ten minutes one or both of you may want to discuss something that has been mentioned by the other. **Agree to a time at least thirty minutes later to move into dialogue.** This will permit the **"5 and 5"** to stand by itself and will also give each of you time to reflect upon what each wants to say, and it may get you both out of a reflex or reactive mode. When you meet for the dialogue, try it for no more than thirty minutes (fifteen to twenty may be better at first), and again set the alarm where neither of you can see it but both of you can hear it.

2) **If it's a difficult subject, you might want to tape it** (what I call the "counselor in the home" technique). Later you can replay the tape and discover what you did well and where you became stuck. Often couples say to me, "I wish we had you at home to help us as you would then hear how we really argue, and you could better help us to change our styles." Usually this translates to "then you would really know that most of our problems are my partner's." My response is to suggest that they turn on a tape recorder prior to discussing a tough issue, and I suggest that this may help them to modify their styles, as they will each know that I may listen to the tape in the next session. If it does go badly then we will have the actual data, not reported conversation, to learn from. Now, you can only do this prior to a discussion. Never suggest it part way through a discussion as doing this could be considered a control issue, especially if it seems that you are losing the argument.

3) When you meet to discuss the issue **decide first the amount of time you want to take discussing it.** A lot of people have found that after twenty to thirty minutes they drop from fairly good dialogue to negative monologue. They move from listening and sharing to stating

and bullying, and from friends to antagonists. Each is often trying to force their individual point of view upon the other, and the other has now become someone who is lacking in "........." As I said earlier, it often helps to set an alarm where neither of you can see it so that you are not distracted by watching the time in order to get the last word in. If the issue is resolved in this time, great. If not, then at the end of the agreed upon time, decide when you will next meet to continue the conversation. Fix an actual time—tomorrow at noon is fine, but just tomorrow or later are not. A lot of couples have found that they can resolve issues if they go for ten twenty to thirty minute sessions rather than a two to three hour marathon.

4) Another tool that I have found helpful is at **about every fourth session, it helps beforehand to write out 1) this is what I am trying to say; 2) this is what I think my partner was trying to say.** This is valuable for a number of reasons:

a) It equalizes power somewhat. When we are sharing orally, one person—the first to share—makes herself or himself vulnerable and the other may never be so vulnerable. When we each write out and begin by exchanging what we have written, and each reads what the other has written before we begin orally, then we each at least know where the other is coming from.

b) Before I give you what I have written, I can redo it as many times as I need to in order to clarify what I am trying to say. When I say it and then regret what I say and ask you to forget it, that just doesn't happen.

c) When I read what you have written, I am more likely to checkout what you meant if what I read is not clear to me. For some reason, when I hear the same thing, I assume I know what you mean and rarely check it out. Sometimes we discover that our disagreement is over mis-understood meanings, not over different opinions on a certain issue.

- Agree to a ten-minute, uninterrupted period every day.
- Toss a coin—winner shares for five minutes, partner listens.

- Interruptions only to clarify.
- Set an alarm for five minutes—when it rings, change roles.
- Second person shares on a totally different topic.
- Alternate starting.
- The person whose turn it is to share first makes sure "5 and 5" happens.
- Don't nag your partner if s/he forgets—you make sure you don't forget!
- Have at least a thirty minute break before any discussion of "5 and 5" topics.

Countdown to a Playful Relationship

REGULAR PLAY	=	COMMUNICATION
3, 2, 1		10

Three	Hours a month	
	(.4% of one month)	
	Hours a week	
	(1.8% of one week)	
Two	Days a year	Ten minutes every day
	(.5% of one year)	(.7% of one day)
One	Week every five years	
	(.4% of five years)	

YOU HAVE THE TIME

CONCEPT

Play

Leads

Into

Talking

5

Positive Playful Manipulation

If you want your partner to do it first, you might have to wait a long time!

If you wait for your partner:

-to plan the date

-to give you a hug

-to say something nice to you

-to affirm your personality

-to appreciate your behavior

-to cook you a special meal

-to surprise you sexually

-to (you fill in the gap)

you might wait a long time!

The secret to receiving is giving! Sadly, we are all acquainted with this in a negative way. We are probably very skilled at the art of negative manipulation, and often, without even having to think about it, we upset, annoy, frustrate, hurt, and anger our partner. The one we say we love is also the one we are able to hurt, and we rarely have to be creative in this area.

Now what if we were to really put our love into action? What if we very intentionally did those things that would please our partner?

+ If I plan the date, and let my partner know well in advance, we will probably have a good time together.

+ If I give my partner a hug, I will also get one.

+ If I say something nice to my partner, s/he will probably say something nice to me.

+ If I affirm my partner, s/he may also affirm me.

+ If I let my partner know that I appreciate her/his behavior then s/he may begin to appreciate me.

+ If I cook my partner a special meal then we can both enjoy the meal and the special time together.

+ If I surprise my partner sexually, I might find lovemaking even more enjoyable.

+ If I (you fill in the gap), I might be pleasantly surprised.

And, if the second part doesn't happen, you can still feel good that you did your part, which is a lot better than feeling resentful because your partner didn't make the first move. Please, don't play the dangerous game of "prove that you love me," or "I'll do it after you." Again, I can't make someone else, and that includes my partner, do anything. And my partner doesn't have to prove her/his love for me. But I can show as often as possible my love for my partner. And if we both have that attitude then we have a win-win situation. All that I have control over is what I do, not what my partner does.

What is love?

Love then means that I will do loving things for my partner, regardless of what s/he does or doesn't do, and regardless of how I feel. I can act lovingly even if I do not feeling loving (remember feelings follow behavior). This is commitment.

Jesus gave us the Golden Rule, which encourages us to treat others in ways we would prefer they treat us. In marriage, I humbly suggest that sometimes this may need a minor revision.

Our experience

Joan and I had not been married very long when Joan was ill and confined to bed for a few days. I applied the Golden Rule and did for Joan what I would want her to do for me. I left her alone. Then a few months later, I was ill and in bed for a few days, and Joan did for me what she had hoped I would have done for her. She came and sat with me and kept me company.

Some time later we both told each other that we had not felt cared for when we were each ill. Joan felt abandoned and I felt pestered. So we asked, "What would you like me to do for you when you are ill in the future?" Joan said, "Come and sit with me and talk to me, or read the paper to me; tell me what's going on." I said, "Give me a bell in case I need anything, otherwise please leave me alone and let me sleep." Reverse Golden Rule.

So then how do we practice Positive Manipulation—how do we put love into action?

"Do for your partner what s/he wants done to/for her/him in order to feel loved by you."

Ask your partner: "What can I do to show my love for you?" The response needs to be clear, practical and easy to evaluate. "Be more helpful" doesn't really tell us very much, and will at best probably result in applying the Golden Rule. "Please put your dirty clothes in the clothes hamper." "Please don't let the gas drop below a quarter in the car." "Please help me write this Christmas letter." (Guess what time of year I am writing this chapter?)—all of these are clearer and thus easier to do and to evaluate and to be appreciated for doing.

Now does this mean that if I ask my partner how I can demonstrate my love that I have to do all that my partner says? Absolutely not! Your decision to do it or not will be based upon a number of factors. For example, if your partner has an alcohol or eating problem and s/he asks for some alcohol or unhealthy foods, your loving response would be to say, "No, but suggest something else I could do for you that would not be harmful to you." If what you are asked to do goes against your beliefs or your morality then you would probably say no. By the way, those kinds of requests are usually indications that your marriage is in big trouble, and that you probably need to seek marital therapy, together!

Your decision to do what is requested needs to come out of your desire to show your partner how much you really love, care, appreciate her/him. And if you are not going to.........then don't say that you will. To say yes and not to do it really creates a big question mark over whether you really love your partner or not.

Now, what if you started every month by asking this loving question of your partner? Imagine that as you go through the month you are each working intentionally at putting your love into action in a way that is easily recognized and appreciated by your partner. Richard Stuart developed this concept at length in his book *Helping Couples Change*, Guilford, 1980. In chapter six, he outlines how to create what he calls "Caring Days."

Love in action

To start this process (I have taken some of Stuart's recommendations and modified some of them), you each draw up a list of twenty to thirty things that you would like your partner to do, that if s/he did some of the things on your list, you would feel loved and cared for. Then you exchange your lists and you each choose two things from your partner's list to work on in the next month. The next month you add (not substitute) two more and so on each month. If there are things on your partner's list that you do not want to do then just ignore them—you don't have to have a discussion with your partner about them. Why twenty to thirty not two or three? Because most of us don't like to be told "Do this!" We want a choice.—I want to make it my gift that I have chosen to give to you. And it prevents either partner saying, "You are only doing this because the counselor suggested it." Let me give you another word of caution. Don't begin with what you think would be number one on your partner's list. Start with something simple, easy to do and that your partner will immediately notice. Make it an action that you can do fairly easily and that, with just a little bit of effort, can become a good habit. Some couples tell each other what the two things are that they are going to do. Others **add this to the play and create a guessing game**—"tell me when you have discovered what I am doing." Either way is fine. Just do it!

How this worked for one couple

Samantha, after being given this exercise, asked Mary Ann, her partner of five years, if she would mind putting gas in her car as Sam hated doing that and usually would go to a full service station and pay someone to do it. Mary Ann was totally unaware that Sam felt that way or that she regularly went to full service stations (money, or lack of, was an issue for them), but she did remember many rows when she pointed out to Sam how low her gas was. Sam had been too embarrassed to say anything before. After this they both became much better at asking for what they wanted. They began to argue less and play more!!

Traps to avoid

1) Some couples object to this concept on the basis of "if s/he really loved me, s/he would know just what to do." I continue to be amazed at how many couples still seem to believe in 'selective and convenient marital telepathy'. I say 'selective and convenient' because when I explain how telepathy would work, if it could, no one really wants it, because all of us would be in big trouble! So let's be grateful our partners are not telepathic, and realizing this, let us tell our partner what we want so that s/he can respond lovingly.

2) Be careful of thinking (assuming) you know what men/women want based upon what your parents did that worked for them, or what did or did not work for you in a previous relationship. People who are widowed often try to duplicate behaviors, and people who are divorced try something different. All that you know from prior relationships is what did or didn't work in them—you know something about that other person and how the two of you interacted. But this is a new and different relationship. And even in this relationship, what worked last year may not necessarily work this year. Stay present and future oriented—ask, ask, ask!

3) Another trap to beware of is the 'gender predictable' one. All men do not act the same, nor do all women! Toni Schindler Zimmerman and Shelley A. Haddock[1] reviewed the research and remind us that our differences are more likely based upon social conditioning than on biological factors. The media and popular literature and entertainment continue to present the myth of gender differences and so continue to justify an inequality of power between men and women. We all have learned behaviors, but these are not set in concrete. Some men/women have learned to behave in a certain way and others the exact opposite. In our relationship I am more comfortable with touching and sharing

---

1.   Toni Schindler Zimmerman and Shelley A. Haddock of Colorado State University and Christine R. McGeorge of the University of Minnesota presented a paper on this topic in the *Journal of Marital and Family Therapy*, January 2001, Vol.27, No.1, p. 55–68.

feelings and Joan is more rational. I would rarely ask for directions if we were lost and Joan does. We fit some of the popular myths and we contradict others. And we have both moved to middle positions on most of these issues—yes, I do sometimes stop and ask directions and sometimes without even being prodded. We can all change; gender behavior is not preset. We can all put love into action and surprise our partner and ourselves.

It's up to you

Positive Manipulation. Why not give it a try? You have nothing to lose!

But, let's not stop there. Let's add a bit more to it. **Let's add a competitive game of "do it before it's done to you."**

We have a choice in marriage—we can be coaches or cheerleaders. Now I have to confess that I am not into sports so if my next few comments are out of line or inaccurate then please forgive me, but try to understand the concept. My understanding and limited observation of coaches at many sports is that they use tough love tactics and withhold praise until it is "well deserved," and they are very free and loud with the criticism—apparently working on the assumption that you can shame people into doing better! Then there are the cheerleaders who are supposed to make everyone on the team feel special telling each member in a variety of ways how great s/he is! Unfortunately, in a lot of the marriages that I work with, I find that I am working with two coaches. What if we decided to become cheerleaders to each other?

Another essential skill

The Marriage Enrichment Movement that David and Vera Mace started includes in their program a technique called "Daily Affirmations."[2] I

---

2.   David and Vera Mace, *How To Have a Happy Marriage,* (Abingdon 1977), p. 125

have adapted their ideas, and what I recommend is that each day we let our partner know what we appreciate about her/him. We don't just say, "I love you" (which is important to say), but we tell each other what that means. It is very important to tell each other specifically what we like about each other, the positive reasons why we are still together, and the funny, endearing and sometimes annoying characteristics that we enjoy. Again try to do it before your partner does. **Another playful activity!** This way we are helping to build up each other's self esteem. We are developing perpetual polite playfulness. You can also include teasing, tickling, sharing humor, smiling at each other, hugs, kisses, etc.

Sometimes when I go away on a trip, I will open my suitcase and as I am unpacking, I will find a love note between my clothes. When Joan goes on a trip, she will sometimes leave a note under my pillow or on the bathroom mirror. She did this first and did it quite a few times and then I began doing it for her. Neither of us do it every time—but I always look for the note and feel great when it is there, and I let her know how good it makes me feel.

- Love means doing.
- You can go first.
- Ask how you can show love to your partner.
- Develop a list of twenty to thirty Loving Actions your partner could do for you. Be specific not vague or general. Exchange lists.
- Choose two a month from your partner's list and do them. Add two more next month, and so on.
- Avoid marital telepathy. Don't assume—ask
- Don't generalize about people—you are each individuals, different and unique.
- Become your partner's cheerleader.

- Share Daily Affirmations.

- Develop perpetual polite playfulness!

CONCEPT

Do it first

Practice

Positive

Playful

Manipulation

Let's Review the Program

1) Play

a) Three Hour Dates

- At least one date a month (preferably one a week).

- Interactive play (not meals or movies).

- Only the two of you.

- Decide a regular (if possible) two to three hour period.

- Toss a coin—winner plans the date (not what your partner would hate).

- Alternate the planning.

- Both intentionally try to enjoy the date (pretend it is with a new person).

- At the end of two months of weekly dates, evaluate.

- Put future date times (at least once a month) in the calendar for the year.

- Keep the commitment.

b) Two Days/Weekend Every Year

- Friday after work to late Sunday night (modify for different schedules).

- Only the two of you.

- Adapt to your financial situations.

c) One Week Every Five Years

- An option—bonus.

- Only the two of you.

- Pamper yourselves.

2) "5 and 5" Playful Sharing Every Day

- Agree to a ten-minute, uninterrupted period every day.

- Toss a coin—winner shares for five minutes, partner listens.

- Interruptions only to clarify.

- Set an alarm for five minutes—when it rings, change roles.

- Second person shares on a totally different topic.

- Alternate starting.

- The person whose turn it is to share first makes sure "5 and 5" happens.

- Don't nag your partner if s/he forgets—you make sure you don't forget!

- Have at least a thirty minute break before any discussion of "5 and 5" topics.

3) Positive Playful Manipulation

- Love means doing.

- You can go first.

- Ask how you can show love to your partner.

- Develop a list of twenty to thirty Loving Actions your partner could do for you. Be specific not vague or general. Exchange lists

- Choose two a month from your partner's list and do them. Add two more next month, and so on.

- Avoid marital telepathy. Don't assume—ask.

- Don't generalize about people. You are each individuals, different and unique.

- Become your partner's cheerleader.

- Share Daily Affirmations.

- Develop perpetual polite playfulness!

Think of this as a house:

The foundation is Play.

The walls are Communication.

The roof is Positive Playful Manipulation.

Implementing the Program

Reading about a good idea is a possible beginning to change. Going to counseling, a retreat or a seminar and hearing from an expert can all be aids to change. When couples come to me for counseling I tell them that twenty percent of the healing may happen in my office but the crucial eighty percent can only happen after they leave. Will they implement what they have heard and are learning?

Another statement that we often hear is "no pain, no gain." I have never really liked that statement as I think it is only partially correct. For many people, it is true that their change and growth came after an event that caused them pain. But this is not so for everyone and it doesn't have to be so. Change can happen because we want it to, because I want something better for myself and we want something better for ourselves.

Therapy is often a painful process but parts of the process can also be pleasant. If people can see the humor in their situations and can begin to laugh at themselves then change may happen. When people come to see me for therapy, they often comment on the fact that they laughed rather than cried! Then when their homework is to play, they are even more surprised. Often I am told that I am oversimplifying their problems. I do not argue. I simply request that they give this program a try. You really can't say it won't work until you have tried it for about six months.

The next section looks at what is needed to apply these great concepts and have them enrich your relationship.

6

Ways to Play & Where to Play

Dr. Herbert Otto recommends developing a 'Surprise Fun Folder.'[1] I would expand this idea and encourage you to develop Play Folders or Play Envelopes. Get a number of file folders or large envelopes. Label them and then fill them with all kinds of play ideas.

Develop folders or envelopes with these and other labels—use your own imagination:

- Indoors play
- Outdoors play
- Serious play
- Silly play
- Sports play
- Hobbies play
- Intellectual play
- Competitive play
- Romantic play
- Sexual play
- Spiritual play
- Summer/Fall/Winter/Spring play
- Play places

---

1.   Dr. Herbert Otto, *More Joy in Marriage*, (Hawthorn Books, 1969)

Remember this is play for just the two of you. Anything else is in addition to your couple playtime.

Still not sure what to do? You like the program—especially the part about your partner planning the play. But you are not sure about what to do when it's your turn! Well, you could ask friends what they do. The likelihood is that they will tell you that they don't do anything, or occasionally they go out for a meal or to a movie. Unfortunately, we are becoming people who are losing the art of play. We are either too busy with our jobs, raising children, or in civic or religious involvement. Or we want canned entertainment at home—television or computer.

How do you fill the folders or envelopes?

- Clip ideas from the newspaper.
- Start creating love-play cards on five by three cards.

Ideas can also come from:

- Radio or television
- Family and friends
- Daydreaming
- Overhearing conversations
- Talks, sermons
- Books, magazines
- Children's play section of the library
- Children's games at the store
- Internet

Both of you can add to the files and envelopes and each of you can choose ideas from them to try. The fact that an idea is there usually means that at least one of you is interested in doing it. You might even want to put one in hoping that your partner will pick it to surprise you.

Now where do we play?

- Almost anywhere.
- At home and away from home.
- Indoors and outdoors.

If you go on business trips and your partner has a flexible job then consider adding on a few days at the beginning or at the end for the two of you to play.

Consider some simply outdoor play such as going for walks in your neighborhood, or try a mystery drive. Get in the car and one of you gives the first direction. Go three blocks and then turn right. The other then gives the next direction, go one mile, or until this road hits a T, and then take the first left. When you get to some interesting place stop and explore. Then try and find your way home!

Joan said to give you some suggestions.

I don't want to give you too many ideas, as I want you to become creative because that's part of what play is. But Joan suggested that it wouldn't hurt for me to give you a few. So let me give you another caution. What is play for one person or couple may not be play for another. Take grocery shopping—is that play or not? It might be dependent on how playfully you do it! If one of you almost always does the shopping alone then it might be fun to do it together at times. At the other extreme, try sex for play.

Try this

John and Andrea told me what they do sometimes. They each clip coupons for a week. Then they go together to a supermarket—shop separately for previously agreed upon items (each can add others as they wish). They then meet in the deli for coffee and to see who the most economical shopper was. Finally they sort out the best buys and together return the rest.

Or this

Ray and Susan have a fantasy sex night every three months. They are a blended family of six years with five teens aged eleven to fifteen. They arrange for all five to go stay with the other parents for a long weekend. They then have the total freedom at their own home to plan meals, activities and sexual fantasies without fear of interruptions. The phone is turned off and the voice mail gets the messages (they check occasionally because of the teens—one of them does not get along with her Dad who she is visiting). One plans one time, the other the next and the third time they develop the fantasy as they go along. They will be in good shape when their kids all leave home.

Well, between fun shopping and fantasy sex, there are a multitude of other activities. Write me about what you discover and maybe I will come up with a book of ideas for couple play. Include in your letter permission for me to print your idea(s). If you are really stuck and can't come up with any ideas at all then check out some of the books that are listed in the Appendix that have hundreds of ideas. But remember the best ideas are the ones that you come up with.

Bedroom

Let me share a few thoughts about the bedroom. It is amazing how many people ruin their bedrooms. They go to bed and lie there looking upwards and have the most fruitless arguments—often finding that part way through one of them falls asleep. It is a really good guideline to have the bedroom off limits for arguments and kept for the adult playroom.

There are some other useful guidelines about the bedroom that Joan and I have learned. Before we were married we were given the advice that many people have been given—don't go to sleep on an unresolved argument. Now this is not good advice and led to much tension for us and for many other couples. The problem is that it worked great for me but not for Joan. I am a night person and so I can continue to discuss things until Joan, who is a morning person, is too tired and just gives in. Well, that's great, until around six am when she wakes me stating I took advantage of her and she wants to reconsider—at that time I will agree to anything in order to get back to sleep. What we came to understand is that we cannot resolve arguments according to a timetable. So we have rewritten the advice to "don't go to bed, and certainly not to sleep, with an unresolved argument before first agreeing when next to talk about it—and leave it outside of the bedroom." For us that means we have to find a time between nine am and nine pm to talk over heavy issues. Now what if something comes up while we are in bed? Acknowledge it and put it on the agenda to discuss tomorrow at six pm. Tomorrow by itself doesn't work. We have to set an actual time, make an appointment, and then keep it.

What if something comes up and you are not willing to wait to discuss it? Then try and make it playful and at least honor the rule of not in the bedroom. What I suggest that you do is move to the bathroom and one of you sits on the toilet and the other in the bathtub or shower and continue the conversation there! Is this yet another way to play?

Keep the bedroom for adult play

CONCEPT

Where to play

How to play

It's as varied as

Your Creativity

7

Obstacles to Working the Program

Okay, now you have the program—what will stop you doing it? Over the years I have heard all kind of excuses and reasons:

- We don't have the time/money.
- I'm waiting to see if you are serious about doing it before I do anything.
- I plan to start tomorrow.
- I'm waiting till I get the urge (or the spontaneous impulse).
- We don't really have the commitment needed.
- I have a resistive partner.

Let's look at these blocks in a bit more detail. We are all somewhat cautious when it comes to making changes so it is normal to have some obstacles to work through.

Time

Now really! What are we talking about here? Let me remind you—I am asking for three hours a month (.4% of each month) as the minimum commitment for just the two of you to have fun. If you can't find this minimal amount of time then I would suggest you look at what is keeping you together. I would also suggest you look at how much time you waste arguing with each other every month. We marry for companionship and if we don't get it by having fun (love-play) then we usually get it the negative way by arguing (combat-play). Add up all the arguing time and next month try something different. Trade in the negative time for positive time—arguing for play. I am still hoping that you will find two to three hours every week (that's only 1.8% of the week).

Ten minutes each day for quality sharing and listening. It really isn't asking very much is it?

I think it makes a lot more sense to take time as a couple to play and stay married, and have a good marriage, than to take even more time individually to play the combat game of divorce, followed by dating someone else. Remember you are older now than when you last dated, and in the 'new couple' one person is still the same—you.

Money

Maybe you are asking, "Can we afford this program?" The question that I have in response is, "Can you not afford it?" Consider the alternatives:

Living with someone you rarely ever have fun with, maybe don't even like all that much. Are you staying together out of a sense of obligation which is quite different from commitment (more on this later)? The price for this approach is often depression or other illnesses or forms of acting-out—all of which have heavy financial consequences as well.

Consider getting a divorce and going through all of those financial expenses and emotional traumas—not only of the actual divorce but also of the ensuing years, especially if you have to continue to share parenting. If you thought it was hard parenting when you lived together, it can be even harder when you are divorced and you have no say as to what happens at the other parent's house.

And what about dating again? Do you remember how much time and energy and money that took before? Well, everything costs more now, and you are older.

If you are really worried about the cost then I invite you to develop a balance sheet. Putting it on paper is often easier than trying to work it out in your head and then trying to discuss vague figures.

On the next page is a suggested balance sheet.

Relationship Balance Sheet

Preventive Costs		_Remedial Costs_	
Weekly Date			
3–4 hours baby-sitting	_____	1-hour counseling	$50–100
Date (see Ch.5)	_____	1-hour attorney	$150–300
		Date with new person	_____
Weekend/Week Away			
Childcare	_____		
Travel, lodging, food	_____		
Entertainment	_____		
"5 and 5"			
No Cost		Phone call to counselor	_____
		Phone call to attorney	_____
		New dating costs	_____

You can implement this program and spend almost nothing or you could make it expensive. It is up to you and your creativity. But don't let money put you off. And don't try to save money by just doing the freebie—**"5 and 5"**. The monthly/weekly play date is the key to this program, and without the key you probably won't get into the house. Regular play usually leads to better conversation, but in my experience and observation of couples good conversation without regular play frequently deteriorates to poor or negative communication.

You do not have to spend a lot of money to impress each other (that's what you do if you end up divorced and dating someone new). In fact, a lot of fun dates don't have to cost anything at all. What about going for a walk in the neighborhood, or maybe you could try the mud/water play.

What about child-care costs? Have you ever thought of getting together with other couples and doing reciprocal child-care? An hour of counseling costs around $100, and an hour of an attorney's time costs even more. For that money you can have a good three hours a month that covers baby-sitting and your creative play activity. And remember you can pay the sitter to have the kids go to the sitter's and you can stay home and save money and have lots of uninterrupted fun!

Many people have documented the financial and health benefits of a good marriage. Linda J. Waite (family sociologist) and Maggie Gallagher (journalist) deal with these and other benefits in their book, *The Case for Marriage*. Linda has based her work on studying hundreds of cross-disciplinary scientific studies. From this they conclude in chapter five [1] that a good marriage can lead to health and happiness and in chapter eight, [2] they go on to add that it can also create a financially secure partnership.

If you want to read more on this then turn on a computer and go to a search engine and type in "effects of marriage on health," and "effects

---

1.　Linda J. Waite & Maggie Gallagher (Broadway Books, 2000) *The Case for Marriage*, p. 64
2.　Ibid p.77

of marriage on finances." In most of this literature, what you will find is that positive results are dependent upon having a healthy relationship. There are, I believe, many hidden financial benefits to developing a playful partnership, which is why again I ask, "Can you not afford to try this program?"

Remember feelings follow actions. So if you want to feel loving then start by doing something loving. In other words, develop what I have already outlined as 'the art of positive playful manipulation.'

I'm waiting to see if you are serious before I do anything

Go back and read all of chapter five—slowly and carefully. It is about you!

Tomorrow

Well, you know what people say about tomorrow. Tomorrow never comes because tomorrow always is tomorrow. The same is true about later. 'I'm a procrastinator' is not a reason—it's a bad excuse! Every procrastinator I have known only procrastinates about some things. And this is often one of them. Let me ask you this: When you were dating, did you say to your present partner, "I'll see you tomorrow/later/sometime next week?" Or did you fix a date (make an appointment) and did you keep it? That same resolve is needed now. You've read this far. So stop reading and start working the program—**now.**

I'm waiting for the spontaneous impulse

Let me tell you a story.

A pastor was appointed to a new church. It was the middle of summer and she was visiting her parishioners. On one of her visits, a couple invited her to sit with them in their garden. It was a beautifully landscaped garden—trees, shrubs, flowers, a pond and a miniature waterfall and a well-manicured lawn. "What a beautiful garden God has given you," said the pastor. "Yes," said the husband, "but you should have seen it five years ago when we moved in, and only God cared for it!"

Marriages, I believe, are a lot like gardens—if you leave them to themselves, they will produce weeds and become overgrown. A beautiful garden is a cooperative project between God and the gardener, and it needs a lot of continual work and care. It is the same with marriages. We have to work at our marriages. If I wait for the spontaneous impulse to work in my garden, then probably nothing will get done. I have to do it whether I want to or not, whether I have the urge or not—unless, of course, what I want is a garden of weeds and dandelions. Marriages will not grow and be healthy if we just wait for the spontaneous impulse to do something.

So, why not put all that time, energy and money into trying to heal your marriage? How? By doing all you can and spending less time complaining about what your partner is not doing or is doing wrong! Remember when you point one finger of blame at your partner three are pointing back to you. Attempts to try to change other people are usually met with major disappointments. My dentist has been trying for years to get me to floss my teeth daily. Sometimes I remember but more often I forget! It is hard for me to change me, but I am the one I am most likely to have the greatest success with.

Love as a feeling follows love as an action. If you wait for the feeling, the spontaneous impulse, you will probably wait too long and begin to feel more and more distant from each other. When you start putting love into action then you will very likely have more spontaneous impulses to do even more!

Lacking commitment

See chapter nine.

I have a resistive partner

Ask. Ask. Ask. If your partner is not open to the idea of playing and having fun with you then you may have to start the program on your own. This doesn't mean that you play by yourself or find someone else to play with. No. It means that you start with positive playful manipulation. You do things for her that will surprise her in a positive way. You melt his coolness with warmth. Maybe you could buy tickets for your partner's favorite pastime (maybe one you don't like) and go with her/him to it and work at enjoying it. Arrange a surprise lunch. Leave love notes and follow up with loving brief phone calls. Take advantage of special days—birthdays, wedding anniversaries, Valentine's Day, holidays, and create an enticement that cannot be refused.

Remember, you cannot make your partner do anything but you can do things to make yourself more attractive to her/him.

If you cannot get your partner's interest and cooperation then I strongly recommend couple counseling before you seriously consider seeing an attorney about divorce. It may help to talk about the possibility of a divorce before you are at that stage. In this way you are not so emotionally hooked into giving up on the relationship. When I am in counseling with a couple who remain stuck after quite a few sessions, I will often suggest that in the next session we talk about what a divorce would mean for them. I carefully explain that I am not suggesting that they get a divorce, only that we seriously address the issue. I may do this even earlier for the couple where one or both use the divorce threat to try to control the other. I continue to be surprised how effective this intervention is. Frequently couples come to the next session unstuck and ready to work the program. Often, in the time between these sessions, they have actually had one or two dates and some have even begun the other parts of the program. To address the subject of divorce when that is the only option left is clearly too late. So talk to your partner about the possibility of a divorce as a way to save the marriage and melt the resistance.

CONCEPT

Where there is

A Will

There is

A Way

8

How to Sustain a Healthy Relationship

A troubled couple

Daphne and Henry came to one of my marriage seminars where I had originally developed these ideas. They had liked the ideas I had presented and had applied them very successfully for about six months. Then they had gradually stopped doing the "**5 and 5**," and they hadn't had a date in a year and a half. They could have just started again on their own as they had purchased the tapes of some of the sessions, but they told me that they thought they needed to see me monthly for accountability.

How to be mutually accountable

Accountability! How do we establish accountability for change as a couple? Some couples can do it with each other by following St. Paul's admonition in Ephesians 5:21—I will let you look up this passage in a Bible and urge you to stick with this verse alone! Others need external accountability. I discovered this over twenty-five years ago when Joan and I met David and Vera Mace and were introduced to the Marriage Enrichment movement (for more information see the Appendix). In 1977, we moved to Winston-Salem, N.C., where David and Vera and ACME were based. While there, we were involved in a number of couples' support groups with three to five other couples—all committed to developing healthy marriages.

Twenty years ago, as I was starting to develop a pastoral counseling practice, I began to specialize in working with couples who were recovering from alcohol or drug addiction. Many of these couples had been in therapy with a variety of therapists over a period of years, going when a crisis emerged and quitting as soon as they 'felt okay.' Over the course of a few months, three or four of these couples came to see me and told me that they wanted to contract to see me not only to work through their crisis but afterwards on a monthly basis. So began what I now call 'grandparent therapy.' Some of these couples I see every month and others every three or six months. We rarely do heavy therapy—they often do that the week before they come to see me. They now have someone they can see for accountability, but not change accountability as in early therapy with a 'parent figure,' but sustaining and growth accountability as with a grandparent.

How then do you sustain and continue your growth as a couple?

Join or start a couples' support group in your faith community, social or civic organization. I don't recommend doing this with people with whom you work. ACME can supply you with materials to help you get started.

OR

Join ACME or a similar organization and join or start an affiliated support group in your area.

OR

Contract with a qualified marriage counselor or pastor for regular 'grandparent therapy.' Give them a copy of this book so that s/he will know what you are working on.

OR

Write to me every three months or so and let me know how you are doing. This would be an absolute last resort if you cannot manage any of the above, and probably will not be enough. But I've never had anyone do this so I can't say if it will help or not.

The earlier in your relationship you start applying these principles the sooner they will become habits. But always remember good habits need more work to sustain than bad habits. If you can establish these principles before you have children, it will be easier to continue them if/when children come along. And when the baby is born, don't wait for more than 3 months before resuming the monthly (preferably weekly) dates.

Couples' Support Groups and Play

When we were in our second couples' support group, the group went through a period of dissatisfaction. None of us were really sure what it was all about until someone shared her or his thoughts and feelings. Let's say it was Dave. Dave said that he had begun to not look forward to the first Tuesday night of the month, our group night. "What issue will we get into tonight?" "What will it bring up that we will need to talk about for the next few weeks?" He went on to say that this wasn't bad as the group had helped them to surface a number of issues that had been very beneficial to them, and had also provided a safe place for them to risk sharing some things. "But why can't we just spend time chatting and getting to know each in a more relaxed way? When we have shared around the topic for the evening, we have coffee and a piece of cake and then we leave. I would like to get to know some of you better, but Deb and I have not asked one of you out as a couple because we did not want to create a subgroup or cliques. What can we do?" Good for Dave. As we then shared, we found that others of us had had similar reactions. So we decided that the next meeting would be a play night. We would all bring our favorite game that we could share with each other and play as couples. We met at the home of one of our couples that had just purchased some of the new video games that you could play on the television, and guess what? We all wanted to play. Guess which couples the rest of us spent most of the night watching and cheering on? Little did we know that night that we were at the beginning of a whole new way of playing that would turn out to be a very mixed blessing or curse.

The above was not support group policy, and so it definitely wasn't the way we were encouraged to spend our time together. Nevertheless we all stayed longer that night than we had previously. And we all put a time on our calendars to get together for another play night, or to go out for pizza, in addition to our regular couples' support group night. Well, it didn't end there! Our local chapter found out what we did and reported us to the State and the State decided that for the next annual meeting we would spend the whole weekend playing—and we did. Traditional family board games, indoor and outdoor games, and then someone brought one of those giant balls and a play parachute that we all ran in and out of. Don't let anyone try to convince you that working on your marriage is not fun. **We spent a whole weekend—couples having fun and playing. We became like children.**

CONCEPT

Be Accountable

And

Play

Play

Play

9

Commitment

When our daughter, Joanne married Roger, they asked me to "preach a sermon." Here are some of my reflections from the sermon as they relate to commitment.

One of my firm beliefs about marriage is that you need to be good friends first. Then in marriage, you work to become and remain each other's best friend (but not the only friend). How then do you make the move from friends to a couple living together in a healthy, creative relationship? What helps a marriage to grow and flourish?

We live today in a disposable, quick-serve society and unfortunately, some people have put marriage there. A few years ago, a friend of mine who does wedding photographs told me that twice that year he had had a couple who had moved to get the marriage annulled before he had developed the wedding pictures. Do we always walk away when the going gets tough? Marriage in this context can be compared to being on a small boat. Sometimes, the weather is good, and the waters are calm and all is well on board. The passengers are happy and having a good time. Sometimes, though, the weather is stormy, and the waters are rough, and it is hard to stay in the boat, but to jump off the boat would probably be suicidal. It is similar with marriages. We need the commitment to work though the stormy times and to arrive together at a new shore. And **the basis of that commitment**—what we have been dealing with all through this book—**is playing and sharing.**

Definition

We have been looking at ways to develop healthy, creative marriages and relationships. However, I have not given you a definition of a healthy, creative marriage. There are many such definitions out there, and because people are different, what fits for one may not fit for another. Some time ago a group of us (men) were talking about a friend's wife. "Could you imagine being married to *her*?"(negative emphasis) and we agreed that we couldn't and felt sorry for our friend. Then one of the group commented, "But he is happy with her, because he knows things about her that we don't know and that makes them good for each other. And it is a good job that we don't see those things or we would all be fighting for her!" Likewise, definitions are risky. Having stated that maybe you would like to give this one a try.

A healthy, creative marriage is one where you are fairly happy most of the time; and where you feel safe almost all of the time—emotionally, physically, sexually and spiritually.

Now, some people say that the first part is expecting too little and the second part too much. Again, I am trying to be realistic. I don't think that two people can be ecstatically happy with each other all of the time. My recommendation is that if they want to evaluate their relationship then do so over a period of at least a month. I suggest that they ask themselves: "During the last month how many days have you looked forward to being together?" Sixteen out of thirty means that your marriage needs some tender, loving care and attention. Twenty out of thirty is probably average—the relationship needs some tender, loving care and attention. Twenty-five out of thirty means that you have a good relationship that with a bit of extra tender, loving care could be even better. Twenty-seven to twenty-eight out thirty suggests that you have a healthy, creative marriage and you know that you can't take that for granted—ongoing tender, loving care is what keeps the score high. Twenty-nine to thirty out of thirty—now come on are you really being honest? If you are, great. Write a book about how to keep the score consistently that high. If your score is less than fifteen out of thirty over a period of a few months then it sounds like your relationship needs major attention—a lot more play is needed, a lot of tender, loving care and maybe marital therapy.

What about the second part? I continue to struggle with whether to put in **"almost"** or to leave it out because safety is very important in any relationship. Again, I have to ask, "What is realistic?" If it is a healthy, creative relationship then I do believe that each person will feel physically safe all the time. Each will know that though both may get angry neither will become violent. Sexually we will not take advantage of each other. Spiritually we will respect each other's beliefs, and even seek to use our differences as opportunities for growth. Emotionally is where I still say "almost all of the time." Most of us will say and do things that cause emotional pain to our partner, but hopefully not very often nor in a premeditated way. A healthy, creative marriage is not devoid of conflict, and we may even come to welcome conflict as a way to celebrate our differences. It is often in our differences that we demonstrate our acceptance of and our commitment to each other. Unfortunately, as I said in chapter five, we are all far better at negative manipulation than we are at positive manipulation.

What am I committed to?

I am committed to making my marriage as positive as I can, and if my partner is committed in the same way, we are on a good path. Sometimes people ask me, "How much do I need to put into my marriage?" They are asking about effort, energy, etc. I used to say that if you each put in fifty percent then you would have a one hundred percent relationship. One of my supervisors in the Department of Pastoral Counseling, N.C. Baptist Hospital, Winston-Salem, Dr. Ted Dougherty, heard me say this in one session with a couple and he then asked me, "Why only fifty percent? If each put in eighty percent then they would have a one hundred and sixty percent relationship." So now I ask folks,

"What would it take for you each to put eighty to one hundred percent into your relationship?"

Commitment means that we want the best for each other and for ourselves. Let us introduce our partner in this positive way. What am I getting at? One of my irritations with people comes out when someone says, "I would like to introduce you to my better half," or "I am sorry that my better half is not here as I know you would really like her/him." Now think about these comments for a moment. On the surface, they sound like you are giving your partner a compliment. But what are you saying about yourself? Are you really only half a person without your partner? Do you really intend to put yourself down? Commitment means that I introduce my partner and myself as whole and healthy.

In marriage I like the math of 1+1=3. There are two whole persons interacting with each other. In the wedding service we often have a unity candle ceremony. The bride and groom take two small candles, these represent their individual lives, and with them they light the third bigger candle, which represents their lives together as a couple. All three need to burn in order to every day relight and reignite the love and passion that each has for the other. This can also be represented by two circles that intersect each other to create three circles—two whole people and a whole, healthy, creative relationship.

Here is an example of what commitment means for some couples.

Credo of an Enriched Marriage

WE HEREBY DECLARE AND AFFIRM

1. That our relationship results from our choices of one another and our ongoing commitment to that choice.

2. That we are married because we are co-creators of our life and not victims of it.

3. That our marriage is created by us with God's help, here and now.

4. That we have a dream about us, which constantly changes; a vision about where we are going and what we are becoming.

5. That within the natural limitations of human experience we will ACT to make our dreams come true.

6. That we will constantly feed our changing relationship with new dreams and hopes and aspirations.

7. That our marriage will never be taken for granted. We will care for, nurture and maintain it as our most precious possession.

8. That we will live intentionally, taking responsibility for what happens to us, boldly shaping what we can of our life, never allowing ourselves to become passive or our relationship accidental.

9. That we will live our relationship powerfully and passionately.

10. That we offer our marriage as a sign of hope to the world of the possibility for the fulfillment of love.[1]

I invite you to finish writing this chapter.

Each of you writes out what commitment means for you as it relates to your marriage. Then get together and create a statement between you about commitment. And then, if you are willing, send me your finished project and I may use it in my next book (with your permission).

---

1.   Quoted by permission from the *Growth in Marriage for Newlyweds* program developed by ACME.

CONCEPT

Commitment

An Ancient

Value

Essential for

Today

PROGRAM POSSIBILITIES

The human race is composed of unique, different and yet similar people. Because of our differences one program will not work for everyone. This final section looks at how the program can help people come to their own decisions about what to do regarding their relationship. Some may need to do other preliminary work before they can successfully implement the program. And a few might discover that in trying to work the program they are really not suited for each other, or they have grown too far away from each other. They will need to decide what the most loving thing is that they can do next for themselves and each other, and if they have children, for the children.

We will then end as we began with a few stories of people who have successfully used these tools and built a creative, growing and playful relationship.

10

If Play Doesn't Heal

What if we do all of this and our relationship does not improve? Well there are a number of other things that I would recommend before you consider getting a divorce.

First, ask yourselves, have we a) really applied the program or b) have we watered it down or c) has one of us either intentionally or unintentionally sabotaged our efforts? If the answer to a) is no; b) or c) is yes then I suggest you reread the book and try again, but this time with a different attitude. If you can't do that then try the next exercise.

Expectations

Maybe you each need to take a careful look at your expectations. I have some guidelines for doing this and again I state that this is an exercise that needs to be written. If for some reason you cannot write then dictate into a tape recorder. There are three parts to this exercise.

1) What I expect out of a spouse. There are three subparts to this: a) the fairy tale, b) the negotiables and c) the non-negotiables. Some of you may be bothered by this concept because you might have heard that people shouldn't have expectations of other people because that will get them in trouble or they will be disappointed. I have never understood these statements. What I see is that a lot of people have problems in relationships because they have unspoken and therefore unshared expectations that get in the way.

a.   The fairy tales. These are the fun hopes/fantasies that we have yet never really expect to be met. But if you never ask, you will probably not get it, and if you ask, you might be surprised. Maybe he is the guy who will give you breakfast in bed on Saturday and Sunday morning. Maybe she is the gal who will change the oil in the cars. Be open to being surprised!

b.   The negotiables. These are those qualities or activities that would mean a great deal if my partner had or did but we can negotiate—compromise. They are more realistic than the fairy tales—they are certainly possible and realistic, but are they reasonable to expect of my partner—do they fit her/his personality?

c.   The non-negotiables. These are what I have to have in order to stay in the relationship. And they are not negotiable! What does that mean you ask? It means without...we have no relationship. It means if you...then we have no relationship!

The above need to be very practical, easily understood and if provided, it will be obvious. "Be more nurturing" is not at all clear. "Give me a hug when I get home from work" is. "Be more supportive" is not clear. "Listen to me without interrupting and giving advice when I tell you I need to share a problem or struggle with you" is.

Suppose one of you is a recovering alcoholic. Then it might be non-negotiable for your partner to continue to be a social drinker if you decided to live together or be married. For another recovering alcoholic this might be negotiable. Having the same religious faith or political beliefs might be non-negotiable for one person and it might be negotiable for another. For most people physical violence is non-negotiable and then when it happens they forget the rule and let it become negotiable, often with devastating consequences. Physical violence should mean that the relationship would end until the batterer has done all possible to prevent violence ever happening again. Be very careful what you say is non-negotiable for that means just what it says!

I recommend taking a few weeks to do your lists and then sit down in a comfortable place where you will not be interrupted. Take 30 minutes to share your lists and discuss what you have written. Don't rush this. It may take a few 30-minute sessions to go through each other's lists and be fair to each other. If something is not clear then take time to clarify it. If what you are expecting is not something your partner is willing to work on or your non-negotiables are not being met then that might explain why the play program did not work for you, and might help you to come to a decision about what you need to do next. But read on. There are still a few other things you can try.

2) Assuming that you are in reasonable agreement on the above, I now suggest that you write out **what I expect out of marriage**. This is not as practical as the above and often includes philosophical ideas like "growing old together," "sharing equally in the raising of children," etc.

3) What I am willing to try to change. Now it is important that this be willingly not grudgingly, and that it does not mean that I give up who I am. We are all very good at telling our partner what s/he needs to change for the marriage to work and we know how unsuccessful this approach is. Remember what I said in chapter seven—when we have one finger pointing at someone else then three are pointing back at me. I am the only person that I can really change, and only I know how hard that is! Then I ask for my partner's help in making these changes.

Again take time and share and discuss two and three with each other. Hopefully this will put you both in a better place to go back and work on the play program with a renewed hope for the improvement of your relationship.

If you are still in a bad space then what? Try this:

Trial separation for the sake of the relationship

It is important that you take in all that the heading states. This is a concept that I had a hard time with twenty years ago. Then, when I heard couples talk of a trial separation, I thought that one of them was just trying to ease the other gently into a divorce. And sometimes this is the case, but not always. To use separation as an easy way into divorce is not fair to either of you. But as an attempt to avoid divorce and to see if the marriage has a chance, it is worth doing this. How long for? At least three months. Yes, you've guessed that I do have a number of suggestions as to how to go about doing this.

To do this successfully takes careful planning and it will cost some money. You need to do it as similar to a divorce as possible. Ideally this means that you will live as if you were divorced. You will each have your own place and not live with family or friends. If you have children you will make the appropriate arrangements for which parent they live with and how visitation is managed. You will have minimal contact with each other—the same as you would if you divorced. Part of the purpose of this exercise is that you can begin to experience what it is like to be divorced so as to see if this is what you really want. If you have children, you may need to contact each other if things come up about the children, but avoid getting into the polite "how are you doing" conversations. And don't keep looking for reasons or excuses to phone. You will work out financial support, how to pay the bills, etc. One of you may have to get a job, one or both of you may have to consider getting a second job, or changing the job you have (for example, if you work together, or you have to alternate jobs in order to manage child-care). This is not a divorce and neither of you will get involved with anyone else during this time. If you do—well, that tells you exactly where you are! My advice is to avoid being alone with a friend or colleague of the opposite sex during this time (if you are homosexual then adapt this suggestion)—you are far too vulnerable in spite of telling yourself that you are different from everyone else that I have worked with. Don't risk it. Drop your narcissism for three months.

During this time I strongly recommend that you each keep a journal in which to put down thoughts, feelings, and reflections. During the first month one person is usually very relieved to be apart and the other is angry. In the second month the first one often finds that being apart (a single person or a single parent) is not so great, and the other starts to find some benefits. In the third month it may begin to even out for each of you. Now this is not a magical timeline, just something that I have observed in a lot of couples. The journal is also the place to put down your thoughts and feelings about being married. Are you enjoying being single, do you miss being married, do you miss being married to your partner, or are you pleased not to be with that person, but aware that you prefer marriage to being single? It takes time to really sort through all of the different permutations. If you have strong urges to phone or contact your partner, resist them and journal. Verbal contact clouds your thinking and feeling, and physical contact will often set the process back days or weeks. You know what it is like being together. This is the time to find out what it is like being apart.

When there are children and/or teenagers then the couple usually meets in my office once a month to deal with issues around the children. Otherwise we set another counseling appointment at the end of the separation period.

My experience is that this needs at least three months. To shorten this usually leads to a premature decision, and if it is to move back together, it can start an on/off pattern that is unhealthy for everyone. Some people need more than three months.

It took two years for one couple

One couple that I worked with took two years. They had been married around twenty-five years in a male dominated marriage that he used scripture and his pastors to reinforce. Sheila had stayed home all this time and raised the children, largely by herself as Tom was working in his job or at his church. He was verbally abusive and controlling and frequently told her what a bad wife and mother she was. She had begun reading some Christian books on marriage and also had made some new Christian friends and joined a women's Bible study group at a different church. She insisted they get some counseling! His pastor referred them to me—the first referral I had ever had from this pastor. After the first session with them, I decided that I probably would not get any more referrals from this source!

After a number of sessions we were stuck. He was sure he was doing nothing wrong and Sheila was not willing to live any longer with what they had. But divorce was not an option for them. So we explored separating for the sake of the marriage. She did not have a paid job, and had no job specific training outside of the home. He stayed in the marital home (surprise, surprise) with the youngest child and she moved in with some friends. He phoned her every day for the first month—now divorce was an option for her! Tom got the message.

They next talked a month later in my office. She had just secured a job and in a month she would be able to afford to get her own apartment. But he reminded her that that would be the end of the three months and time for her to move back. Not so, and she reminded him that three months was the minimum and she had only just started her journey of nurturing herself and was nowhere near ready to think about the marriage. And, as far as she knew, he had not done anything about getting into individual counseling to work on his personal issues. He now got serious and began working on his issues—including finishing a lot of jobs around the house and property. After one year they began to meet weekly for a date, and after six months of dating they went away together for a weekend, and after a further six months they met with their pastor and exchanged some new marriage vows that they had written, and moved back together.

At the end of the separation the couple meets in my office. Sometimes they already know what each wants, and sometimes this is an anxious time, as neither knows what the other now wants. Clearly there are more permutations for staying apart than there are for reuniting. To reunite really has to be something that both wants. When this happens I find that they move from blaming the other and telling the other what to change, to each taking responsibility for what each can do differently or better to make the marriage work. What are the reasons for this decision? Well, there are many and they are all okay. It doesn't matter if one wants to get back because s/he has missed their partner and the other wants to get back for the sake of being a united family. Love by itself will not heal the relationship. It will take commitment, time and energy. It will involve love not as a feeling but as an action and this is very possible regardless of the motivation.

If the relationship still isn't working?

What if after all this the decision is to divorce? Again, my experience with these couples is that they are more able now to work through a fairly friendly divorce, even in cases where one wants to reunite but the other doesn't. They are now less angry at each other, and they each know that they have both been seriously trying to work this out. They are usually less reactive.

Counseling

What about counseling? This is a good idea but make sure that what you get is couple counseling with someone who is trained in this field. Most counselors, social workers, psychologists, psychiatrists have had some courses in couple/marriage counseling and some have specialized in this area. Look in the yellow pages under counselors/marital therapists and look for a listing under American Association for Marriage and Family Therapy (see Appendix) and look for people whose state credential is the MFT license. If you want a therapist who will work with spiritual issues and respect your beliefs then contact the American Association for Pastoral Counseling (see Appendix).

Ask about training, experience, fees, availability out of sessions (how they manage crises); how often they do continuing education and in what areas; do they meet regularly with other therapists for case sharing and consultation and/or supervision; what is their policy regarding psychiatric referrals; do they see you only as a couple or do they do individual sessions (I very, very rarely see couples individually as I do not want to receive information about the other without that person being present and I do not want to create alliances or add to distrust, etc). My first session is always with the couple, unless it is a case of domestic violence. If someone believes that s/he needs to come in alone to tell the therapist certain things then s/he would not see me. For the reasons for seeing someone individually to work on the relationship see Michele Weiner-Davis' book, *Divorce Busting.*

Does the therapist need to see you every week and if so why? Weekly therapy, I believe is usually for the benefit of the therapist not the client and this is especially true for couple therapy. Weekly therapy is expensive, creates too much dependency upon the counselor, does not give enough time between the sessions to do homework, and makes it harder for the counselor to know how motivated you are. If you do not do the homework with a two or three week spacing you may be expecting the therapist to work magic for you. What I tell couples is that twenty percent of the healing takes place in my room—the crucial eighty percent takes place outside of it.

Ask friends who they have been to. Ask your pastor, your doctor, etc. But a word of caution: a really good recommendation means that that therapist helped your friend and they developed a good therapeutic relationship but this may not be so for you, so still ask all your questions and trust your intuition about the therapist. Don't see a therapist who one of you has negative feelings about. If you can't agree on a therapist then that tells you something loud and clear.

If Nothing Works!

How do you go about getting a divorce? I think there are three ways to go.

1) Get a do-it-yourself divorce kit and work on this together. You may decide to enlist the services of a paralegal for help with some of the technical details.

2) Work together with a mediator. These are usually listed in the yellow pages under mediators, or look under counselors for someone who does this work. People who do this work should have had additional training in this field (ask when and where they had training), and they are usually counselors or attorneys. Make sure your mediator has not been barred from their prior profession and are doing this because it is as yet unregulated by most states.

3) You can each hire your own attorney and let them do most of the work for you.

If you do number three, remember you are hiring the attorney. The attorney is working for you. You want to know what the law allows and you want your attorney to ask for what you want, which may not be the same as what the attorney "tells" you that you should go for. Clients who have gone through this experience recommend asking for what you want at the beginning to prevent having to go back to court years later to try for a modification. You will have to live with this for the rest of your life—your attorney won't. Ask all the questions you need to before you select the attorney to represent you—experience, fees, how soon does s/he return phone calls, what is her/his policy regarding you being in court, will s/he give you a regular summary of your account, do you feel that you are being treated with respect as a person or just another client—a number.

But

Have you really tried to play with each other?

CONCEPT

You

Always

Have

Choices

11

Stories of Hope

Diane and Susan's story

Diane and Susan had been in a committed relationship for sixteen years. For the last three years there had been constant arguing and increased distancing. Diane would yell and blame and accuse, and Susan would cry, apologize and then clam up. This resulted in Diane becoming even angrier and often storming out of the house, and staying away for some time. After one of these incidents, she was gone for four days.

Early in the first session I asked what had and was keeping them together. They both stated that primarily they were together because of their two adopted children. Also they had gone through a great deal of stress with their families, friends and their church in order to be accepted as a couple. Each of them stated that she believed it was important to demonstrate that committed lesbian relationships can work. But they no longer liked or respected each other and the climate at home was not a good one for their children to be raised in. In public they maintained a good image but they paid the price when they closed the doors of their home.

At the end of the first session I gave them the alternate dating assignment. When they came back two weeks later they were in worse shape. They had managed to argue over how to do the coin toss, and so they had not had a date! We processed that and then I suggested that they try to do the expectations exercise. Session three:—Susan had done the exercise but Diane had not had time to do it. Susan, the passive one, was now angry and expressing her anger. She couldn't see any point in continuing the relationship. Diane agreed. As we talked about what splitting permanently would mean they both stated that they didn't want that, so they decided to do the three months separation, agreeing to meet in my office at the end of each month to work on child related concerns. We also agreed to meet at the end of the three months to see where they were regarding what to do about their relationship. Each of them stated that they wanted to do some individual counseling during the separation. I left them to find their individual counselors.

Going into the waiting room after their three-month separation, I was aware of a change, such that I had noticed before with similar couples. They each looked relaxed and when they spoke they sounded different. Their voices were softer and they were smiling. No longer were they blaming each other. In fact, each was saying what she was willing to do differently to improve the relationship. However, neither was ready to move back together. They wanted to get to know each other without the stress of living together. Above all, they wanted to do the two months intensive dating and to take an anger management class together.

Three months later they had a big party and moved back together. They had their pastor lead them in a recommitment ceremony. We continued to meet every two weeks for the next two months and then monthly for the next six months as we monitored their growth and established patterns of accountability. They continue to see me yearly for ongoing accountability.

Prior to moving to the monthly sessions we reviewed their progress. They both stated that what they discovered had happened in their relationship was that they had stopped playing and having fun with each other. After they adopted the children, they focused so hard on being a family that they lost their couple-ness. When they were separated they each began playing with other friends and realized that they used to do that with each other, and that that had been a large part of what had drawn them to each other. When they first met they had similar fun interests, and now they again discovered that they still had those interests and some new ones. Reconnecting for them meant not moving back together until they had rediscovered and affirmed their friendship. Living together successfully meant being intentional about having weekly play, daily fun, giving each other regular affirmations and sharing playful moments.

Dave and Isabel's story

Dave and Isabel had had a wonderful forty-six years of marriage. They had five adult children, eleven grandchildren and three great-grandchildren that they loved and spent a lot of their free time with some of them. That was the strength and weakness of their relationship. For the last thirty-five years, Dave had been in a job that took him away for six to eight weeks at a time. Then he would be home for one to two weeks. As they put it, "It was like we had a honeymoon every few months." She was busy with raising the children, being involved in their school and other child related activities, and she was also active on a number of community boards. When he came home, he connected with the family as best he could.

Four of the children married before they were twenty and bought or rented homes in the area and quickly had their own children. Isabel was happy. She was a grandmother with a sizeable family to look after. And Dave—he just continued to fit in as best he could! That was until he retired. Two of their grown children had moved to the east coast and their three great-grandchildren were there. Of the three that were near Dave and Isabel, two were divorced and the third had never had a significant relationship but had a very good job and was content living on his own. All of the grandchildren were now in their late teens or early twenties. Family events did not happen as often. Frequently, Isabel and Dave were at home by themselves for days with no visitors. What were they to do? They were not used to being alone together for so long.

After two years of complaining and blaming, they decided that they had nothing in common, nothing to talk about and that they were incompatible and needed therefore to get divorced. In their forty-six years together they had been more used to being apart than together. When they told their kids, they were horrified. One of the sons, who was divorced, had been in marriage counseling with me ten years before and so he strongly suggested that his parents come in to see me. Reluctantly, they agreed. Neither of them were the counseling type. They believed in taking care of their problems by themselves.

As I listened to their story I heard yet again of a family that many people considered the 'ideal family.' But as they came to dis-cover—take away the children and the grandchildren and they had very little in common. They had ceased being a couple almost forty years ago. I suggested to them that they needed to start all over again from the beginning. They assured me that they were too old to do that. I countered with, "Maybe you are also too old to get a divorce." "You're quite blunt and to the point," said Dave, "and maybe you're right. What do you suggest we do then?" I outlined for them the con-cept of "Intensive Alternate Dating." Neither of them was sure that they could do this. They certainly saw the wisdom of it and wished that someone had suggested it to them forty-six years ago, but to start dat-ing in their late sixties!

They returned two weeks later still very unsure about their future together. The first week they had been unable to agree about what to do so they did nothing. Each waited for the other to make a suggestion and neither did until the day before their second counseling session. Dave said, "Let's go for a drive up the Gorge." So they did—in silence all the way there and all the way back.

Now at this point I was tempted to retreat to a more traditional counseling approach and help them look back over their history to dis-cover where they went wrong in order to try to correct it. Instead I complimented them for having had a date, their first in many years, and, I suggested, the first of many yet to come. Then I encouraged them to build on their success. They were hooked. What they had considered a failure I had helped them turn into a success, and hopefully the beginning of many. To help ensure further successes, I took out a coin and tossed it for them, asking Isabel to choose. "Heads," she said, and heads it came down. "Okay, so this week you plan the date, and you, Dave do your best to make it a success and hopefully to enjoy it. And if you aren't enjoying it then fake it, because next week you reverse the roles." By tossing the coin, I was able to review the intensive alternate dating guidelines without appearing to criticize them for not following my earlier instructions.

Session three and they were smiling. Isabel had taken them to an antique auction and had successfully bid on an old chiming clock—Dave loved old clocks. The next week Dave took them to a symphony concert—a real gift of love as he wasn't very musical and Isabel was. He surprised himself by enjoying it. They bumped into some old friends they hadn't seen in years and made plans to meet them the next week. Yes, I know they were still modifying my guidelines. They planned what each thought the other would enjoy. But it was working so I wasn't going to knock it.

Married life began anew for them as they now had weekly dates, enjoyed trips, and took time to reconnect with old friends. They both became active in the seniors group at their synagogue. Isabel became reinvolved in volunteer work in the community and Dave did some consulting. Now they had a healthy balance of individual, couple, and yes, they managed to find time for the extended family events. I saw them about five years after our last session at a local community theatre production. "We're still doing our weekly dates and enjoying being married," said Dave, "and it's good to see that you practice what you teach."

APPENDIX

Referral sources for couple counseling

American Association of Pastoral Counselors, 9504A Lee Highway, Fairfax, VA 22031-2303, (703) 385-6967; email info@aapc.org; www.aapc.org

American Association for Marriage & Family Therapy, 112 South Alfred St., Alexandria, VA 22314-3061. (703) 838-9808; www.aamft.org; www.therapistlocator.net

Yellow Pages—look under the AAMFT listing, or look for therapists who are state licensed as MFTs (Marriage and Family Therapists).

Ask your pastor, doctor, or someone whom you know who has had couple counseling.

Referral Sources for Marriage Enrichment, Support Groups, etc.

Association for Couples in Marriage Enrichment, P.O. Box 10596, Winston-Salem, N.C. 27108; (800) 634-8325; e-mail acme@ bettermarriages.org; www.bettermarriages.org

National Marriage Encounter; (800) 828-3351; www.marriage-encounter.org

World Wide Marriage Encounter; www.wwme.org

Recommended Reading

The Seven Principles for Making Marriage Work, John Gottman, Ph.D., and Nan Silver, Three Rivers Press, 1999

The Relationship Cure, John Gottman et al, Crown Publishing Group, 2001

Divorce Busting, Michele Weiner-Davis, Fireside, 1992

Love Is A Verb, Bill O'Hanlon and Pat Hudson, Norton, 1995

How to Have a Happy Marriage, David and Vera Mace, Abingdon, 1977

Dating Activities Books

Romantic Dates, Gregory J.P. Godek, Sourcebooks, 1997

1001 Ways to Be Romantic, Gregory J.P. Godek, Sourcebooks, revised edition, 1999

The RoMANtic's Guide, Michael Webb, Hyperion, 2000

Couples and the Art of Playing is a great gift for a friend or family member at anytime, but especially as an engagement, wedding or wedding anniversary gift. It is also a wonderful book to give your partner or friend as a Valentine gift.

To order an extra copy or copies, check your local bookstore or contact www.iUniverse.com/bookstore

If you would like Keith to give a presentation or workshop to your organization, church, school, company or association, contact him regarding availability and fees at Keith@KeithHackett.net.

0-595-29102-3